The Writer's Inspirational Notebook

The Writer's Inspirational Notebook

Eden S Gruger

Eccentric Girl Press

© 2021 Eden Gruger. All rights reserved.
ISBN 978-1-7398642-1-7
The right of Eden Gruger to be identified as the author of this work has been asserted by him in accordance with the Copyright, Designs and Patents Act 1988

All rights reserved, no part of this publication may be reproduced, stored in or introduced into a retrieval system, or transmitted, in any form, or by any means (electronic, mechanical, photocopying, recording or otherwise) without the prior written permission of the publisher. Any person who does any unauthorised act in relation to this publication may be liable to criminal prosecution and civil claims for damages

It's time to get your ideas out of your head
and onto the page -

"you cannot finish a book
that you never began" ~ Eden Gruger

"A professional writer is an amateur who didn't quit."
~ Richard Bach

EDEN S GRUGER

"There is no greater agony than bearing an untold story inside you." ~ Maya Angelou

EDEN S GRUGER

"Close the door. Write with no one looking over your shoulder." ~ Barbara Kingsolver

EDEN S GRUGER

"It's a mysterious process, but I hope I never find out exactly how it works." ~ J.K. Rowling

EDEN S GRUGER

"With writing, the way you feel changes everything."
~ Stephenie Meyer

EDEN S GRUGER

"Words can be like X-rays if you use them properly – they'll go through anything. You read and you're pierced." ~ Aldous Huxley

EDEN S GRUGER

"If you wait for inspiration to write you're not a writer, you're a waiter." ~ Dan Poynter

EDEN S GRUGER

"There are three rules for writing the novel. Unfortunately, no one knows what they are." ~ W. Somerset Maugham

EDEN S GRUGER

"You have to follow your own voice. You have to be yourself when you write." ~ David Morrell

EDEN S GRUGER

"[As a writer] you have to have the three D's: drive, discipline and desire. If you're missing any one of those three, you can have all the talent in the world, but it's going to be really hard to get anything done." ~ Nora Roberts

EDEN S GRUGER

"The worst enemy to creativity is self-doubt." ~ Sylvia Plath

EDEN S GRUGER

"A great and interesting story is about everyone or it will not last." ~ John Steinbeck

EDEN S GRUGER

"There's no better teacher for writing than reading... Get a library card. That's the best investment." ~ Alisa Valdes

EDEN S GRUGER

"If you don't have time to read, you don't have the time (or the tools) to write. Simple as that." ~ Stephen King

EDEN S GRUGER

"If there's a book that you want to read, but it hasn't been written yet, then you must write it." ~ Toni Morrison

EDEN S GRUGER

"A word after a word after a word is power."
~ Margaret Atwood

EDEN S GRUGER

"You should write because you love the shape of stories and sentences and the creation of different words on a page. Writing comes from reading, and reading is the finest teacher of how to write." ~ Annie Proulx

EDEN S GRUGER

"I write to discover what I know."
~ Flannery O'Connor

EDEN S GRUGER

"You have to write the book that wants to be written. And if the book will be too difficult for grown-ups, then you write it for children." ~ Madeleine L'Engle

EDEN S GRUGER

"Get it down. Take chances. It may be bad, but it's the only way you can do anything really good." ~ William Faulkner

EDEN S GRUGER

"Read a thousand books, and your words will flow like a river."
~ Lisa See

EDEN S GRUGER

"As a writer, you should not judge, you should understand."
~ Ernest Hemingway

EDEN S GRUGER

"Write what should not be forgotten." ~ Isabel Allende

EDEN S GRUGER

"The story must strike a nerve in me. My heart should start pounding when I hear the first line in my head. I start trembling at the risk." ~ Susan Sontag

EDEN S GRUGER

"I am not at all in a humor for writing; I must write on until I am." ~ Jane Austen

EDEN S GRUGER

"I don't wait for moods. You accomplish nothing if you do that. Your mind must know it has got to get down to work."
~ Pearl S. Buck

EDEN S GRUGER

"There is no real ending. It's just the place where you stop the story." ~ Frank Herbert

EDEN S GRUGER

"I would advise any beginning writer to write the first drafts as if no one else will ever read them — without a thought about publication — and only in the last draft to consider how the work will look from the outside." ~ Anne Tyler

EDEN S GRUGER

"I do not over-intellectualise the production process. I try to keep it simple: Tell the damned story." ~ Tom Clancy

EDEN S GRUGER

"You fail only if you stop writing." ~ Ray Bradbury

EDEN S GRUGER

"The secret to being a writer is that you have to write. It's not enough to think about writing or to study literature or plan a future life as an author. You really have to lock yourself away, alone, and get to work." ~ Augusten Burroughs

EDEN S GRUGER

"Even if you write it wrong, write and finish your first draft. Only then, when you have a flawed whole, do you know what you have to fix." ~ Dominick Dunne

EDEN S GRUGER

"Find your best time of the day for writing and write. Don't let anything else interfere. Afterwards it won't matter to you that the kitchen is a mess."~ Esther Freud

EDEN S GRUGER

"Find enough clever things to say, and you're a Prime Minister; write them down and you're a Shakespeare."
~ George Bernard Shaw.

EDEN S GRUGER

> "Failures are finger posts on the road to achievement."
> ~ C. S. Lewis

EDEN S GRUGER

THE WRITER'S INSPIRATIONAL NOTEBOOK

"All stories have to at least try to explain some small portion of the meaning of life." ~ Gene Weingarten

EDEN S GRUGER

"After nourishment, shelter and companionship, stories are the thing we need most in the world." ~ Philip Pullman

EDEN S GRUGER

"Writers are like dancers, like athletes. Without that exercise, the muscles seize up." ~ Jane Yolen

EDEN S GRUGER

"If you want to change the world, pick up your pen and write."
~ Martin Luther

EDEN S GRUGER

"You can't let praise or criticism get to you. It's a weakness to get caught up in either one." ~ John Wooden

EDEN S GRUGER

"My aim in constructing sentences is to make the sentence utterly easy to understand. I've failed dreadfully if you have to read a sentence twice to figure out what I meant." ~ Ken Follett

EDEN S GRUGER

"Write your story as it needs to be written. Write it honestly, and tell it as best you can." ~ Neil Gaiman

EDEN S GRUGER

"Do not hoard what seems good for a later place in the book, or for another book; give it, give it all, give it now."
~ Annie Dillard

EDEN S GRUGER

"It is perfectly okay to write garbage - as long as you edit brilliantly." ~ C. J. Cherryh

EDEN S GRUGER

"No matter what people tell you, words and ideas can change the world."~ Robin Williams

EDEN S GRUGER

"The very reason I write is so that I might not sleepwalk through my entire life."~ Zadie Smith

EDEN S GRUGER

"You can always edit a bad page. You can't edit a blank page."
~ Jodi Picoult

EDEN S GRUGER

"You don't start out writing good stuff. You start out writing crap and thinking it's good stuff, and then gradually you get better at it. That's why I say one of the most valuable traits is persistence." ~ Octavia E. Butler

EDEN S GRUGER

"Anyone who says writing is easy isn't doing it right."
~ Amy Joy

EDEN S GRUGER

> "The first draft is just you telling yourself the story."
> ~ Terry Pratchett

EDEN S GRUGER

"One thing that helps is to give myself permission to write badly. I tell myself that I'm going to do my five or 10 pages no matter what, and that I can always tear them up the following morning if I want. I'll have lost nothing — writing and tearing up five pages would leave me no further behind than if I took the day off." ~ Lawrence Block

EDEN S GRUGER

"I'm very lucky in that I don't understand the world yet. If I understood the world, it would be harder for me to write these books." ~ Mo Willems

EDEN S GRUGER

"It doesn't matter how many book ideas you have if you can't finish writing your book." ~ Joe Bunting

EDEN S GRUGER

"Start writing, no matter what. The water does not flow until the faucet is turned on." ~ Louis L'Amour

EDEN S GRUGER

"All you have to do is write one true sentence. Write the truest sentence that you know." ~ Ernest Hemingway

EDEN S GRUGER

"Literature is strewn with the wreckage of men who have minded beyond reason the opinions of others." ~ Virginia Woolf

EDEN S GRUGER

"Your writing voice is the deepest possible reflection of who you are. The job of your voice is not to seduce or flatter or make well-shaped sentences. In your voice, your readers should be able to hear the contents of your mind, your heart, your soul."

~ Meg Rosoff

EDEN S GRUGER

"It is only by writing, not dreaming about it, that we develop our own style." ~ P.D. James

EDEN S GRUGER

"To gain your own voice, you have to forget about having it heard." ~ Allen Ginsberg

EDEN S GRUGER

"Ideas are cheap. It's the execution that is all important."
~ George R.R. Martin

EDEN S GRUGER

"Ideas are like rabbits. You get a couple and learn how to handle them, and pretty soon you have a dozen." ~ John Steinbeck

EDEN S GRUGER

"Start before you are ready." ~ Steven Pressfield

EDEN S GRUGER

"You can't wait for inspiration. You have to go after it with a club."~ Jack London

EDEN S GRUGER

"I'm writing a first draft and reminding myself that I'm simply shoveling sand into a box so that later I can build castles." ~ Shannon Hale

EDEN S GRUGER

"I get a lot of letters from people. They say, "I want to be a writer. What should I do?" I tell them to stop writing to me and get on with it." ~ Ruth Rendell

EDEN S GRUGER

THE WRITER'S INSPIRATIONAL NOTEBOOK

"First, find out what your hero wants, then just follow him!"
~ Ray Bradbury

EDEN S GRUGER

"Writing a novel is like driving a car at night. You can only see as far as your headlights, but you can make the whole trip that way." ~ E. L. Doctorow

EDEN S GRUGER

"Never write anything that does not give you great pleasure. Emotion is easily transferred from the writer to the reader."
~ Joseph Joubert

EDEN S GRUGER

"Writing without revising is the literary equivalent of waltzing gaily out of the house in your underwear." ~ Patricia Fuller

EDEN S GRUGER

"Write your first draft with your heart. Rewrite with your head." ~ Mike Rich

EDEN S GRUGER

"Outside of a dog, a book is man's best friend. Inside of a dog, it's too dark to read."~ Groucho Marx

EDEN S GRUGER

"If you can tell stories, create characters, devise incidents, and have sincerity and passion, it doesn't matter a damn how you write." ~ Somerset Maugham

EDEN S GRUGER

"Imagination is everything. It is the preview of life's coming attractions." ~ Albert Einstein

EDEN S GRUGER

"I must write it all out, at any cost. Writing is thinking. It is more than living, for it is being conscious of living."
~ Anne Morrow Lindbergh

EDEN S GRUGER

"Don't try to figure out what other people want to hear from you; figure out what you have to say." ~ Barbara Kingsolver

EDEN S GRUGER

"Turn up for work. Discipline allows creative freedom. No discipline equals no freedom." ~ Jeanette Winterson

EDEN S GRUGER

"A man's got to take a lot of punishment to write a really funny book." ~ Ernest Hemingway

EDEN S GRUGER

"Writing is hard for every last one of us... Coal mining is harder. Do you think miners stand around all day talking about how hard it is to mine for coal? They do not. They simply dig."
~ Cheryl Strayed

EDEN S GRUGER

"Accept bad writing as a way of priming the pump, a warm-up exercise that allows you to write well." ~ Jennifer Egan

EDEN S GRUGER

"It tends to happen when I get out of the way—when I let go a little bit, I surprise myself." ~ Aimee Bender

EDEN S GRUGER

"You probably have time to be a halfway decent parent and one other thing." ~ David Mitchell

EDEN S GRUGER

"You have to simply love writing, and you have to remind yourself often that you love it." ~ Susan Orlean

EDEN S GRUGER

"Work on one thing at a time until finished." ~ Henry Miller

EDEN S GRUGER

If you would like help on the next stage of your author journey the Out of Your Head and Onto The Page Masterclasses answer:

- How To Write (Without Block)
- How To Choose A Publisher?
- Who Is Your Ideal Reader?
- Where To Find Your Ideal Reader?
- Why Do Authors Need A Brand?
- How To Design A Great Cover?
- How To Choose An Editor?
- What Is The Difference Between Marketing And Sales?
- How Writer's Use Social Media?
- How, Where, When to Market Your Book?
- How To Have A Great Author Website?
- How To Approach Bookshops?
- How To Launch Your Book Online and Off?
- How Authors Use A Mailing List?
- How To Give Author Interviews?

Useful links

If you would like to be part of my writer's community, you can apply to join here: facebook/make-your-book-a-reality

Visit the picture writing prompt page

https://edengrugerwriter.online/writing-prompt-pictures/

Writers and artists yearbook forum

https://www.writersandartists.co.uk/community

The Arvon Foundation

https://www.arvon.org/

Subscribe to my FREE weekly KEYS to Publishing emails here

https://bit.ly/2UEbP4M

Alliance of Independent Authors website offers free resources and membership

https://www.allianceindependentauthors.org/?affid=8022

Follow my socials at:

https://www.edengrugerwriter.online/make-your-book-a-reality

twitter/com/edengrugerwrit1

instagram.com/make_your_book_a_reality/

pinterest.co.uk/edengruger/out-of-your-head-and-onto-the-page/

THE WRITER'S INSPIRATIONAL NOTEBOOK

www.ingramcontent.com/pod-product-compliance
Lightning Source LLC
Chambersburg PA
CBHW070900080526
44589CB00013B/1146